Copyright © 2016 by Joan Randall, All rights reserved. No part of this book may be reproduced in any form without the written permission of the author and its publisher.

Acknowledgements

To my husband Bill Randall, the head of our home and my earthly King. In you I found the best of me.

To my children, Kaydene, Shayana, Brianna and Brandon, you are my inspiration.

To Vanessa Smith my Accountability Partner, your encouragement pushed me to deliver. To Barbara Baker Greer thank you for your support.

To my sister Shelly who is my right hand. Thank you for always believing in me.

To Steve and Kathy Kidd, a special thank you.

Introduction

I was a victim of Domestic Violence. I skillfully hid it from my family, friends and the people around me. I was embarrassed, ashamed, prideful, and scared to speak about it. So I kept quiet and endured years of physical, emotional, verbal and financial abuse.

I had no knowledge of the resources that were available to me. I never heard anyone speak publicly in the media about Domestic Violence. As a matter of fact, I never knew, that what was happening to me had a name. I just thought that my husband was mad or angry with me and hurt me as a result. I felt alone, isolated and I suffered in silence.

One day a coworker gifted me with a journal. Little did she know that her gift would provide an outlet for me to speak without opening my mouth. Writing in that journal was my therapy.

That journal had blank lined pages. Although it helped to ease my pain by giving me an outlet to release my thoughts, there was nothing that I could hold onto for daily inspiration. The pages had no quotes or bible verses or encouraging words. So all I did was write what I felt and what I thought.

This book is born out of that experience and is exactly that. I created this Devotional Journal as a medium to provided daily devotion, inspiration, affirmation and hope during difficult times. It also allows you the opportunity to write your thoughts, concerns and reflections on the pages.

If this Devotional Journal was available to me several years ago, I would have experienced a sense of daily encouragement and comfort to lighten those dark days and help me through the most difficult times in my life.

No matter what your circumstances are, no matter the position that you find yourself in at this moment, or how difficult life can be at times, know that Faith and Prayer can take you to places far beyond your physical reach. Faith is like air, you cannot see it but you need it to live. Hope, is knowing that your unfortunate situation is only temporary and Victory is around the corner.

The great thing about the Human Spirit is that it is resilient and durable and can withstand the storms.

Whatever you are going through now, rest assured that nothing lasts forever and this too shall pass. Before long your life will be fulfilled, you will be rewarded and you will be able to give God the praise and recognition he deserves for bringing you through.

Use this Devotional/Journal daily for your morning or evening devotion, to get inspiration, and as your personal writing journal. This book can also be used as a study guide in claiming victory over your circumstances.

"I can do all things through Christ which strengtheneth me" *Philippians 4:13*

This Book is dedicated to my lifelong, childhood, Best Friend Forever, Pauline Fennell.

Day 1
Habakkuk 3:19, KJV

"The Lord is my strength, and he will make my feet like hinds' feet, and he will make me to walk upon mine high places. To the chief singer on my stringed instruments."

No matter what you are going through today, there is power in the name of God. He will cast your enemies under your feet and lift you up to high places. Call on his name and you will find comfort.

"Dear God, Today I ask you for strength. Strength to survive, to overcome, to be victorious. Guide my feet as I walk through this valley and keep me safe and protected. Cast out all fear from my heart and replenish me so that I can walk upright into the place that you have prepared for me. These things I ask in your name. Amen."

Personal Thoughts/Reflections

Day 2
Psalms 18:35, KJV
"Thou has also given me the shield of thy salvation: and thy right hand had Holden me up, and thy gentleness hath made me great."

The Lord is your shield and he will always support and help you. He will open doors no man can close and will elevate you among your enemies.

"Lord, I thank you for placing your shield around me. I ask that you continue to support me and direct my steps. Help me to become all that you desire me to be. I trust and believe in your words. For this I pray in your most Holy name. Amen."

Personal Thoughts/Reflections

Day 3
1 Corinthians 15:57, KJV
"But thanks be to God, which giveth us the Victory through our Lord Jesus Christ."

In everything you do you must give thanks to God for bringing you through your wilderness experiences. Those experiences strengthen your Faith and makes you stronger.

"Holy and Righteous Father, Today I gave you all the praise and glory for bringing me through my storms. I trust that you will continue to lead me Lord. I am grateful that you sent your Son Jesus Christ to die for my sins so that I can have an abundant life. Amen."

Personal Thoughts/Reflections

Day 4
2 Corinthians 2:14, AMP
"But thanks be to God, who in Christ always leads us in triumph (as trophies of Christ's victory) and through us spreads and makes evident the fragrance of the knowledge of God everywhere."

All you need is a little faith, the size of a mustard seed. Believing that God will deliver you and lead you into triumph. This will allow others to see the goodness of his grace in you.

"Lord I thank you for loving me enough to lead me out of the battle into victory. Thank you for your grace and mercies and for seeing it fit to adorn me with your blessings. Amen."

Personal Thoughts/Reflections

Day 5
1 Samuel 17:47, KJV

"All those gathered here will know that it is not by sword or spear that the Lord saves; for the battle is the Lord's and he will give all of you into our hands."

Our closest friends, family members, and loved ones tends to hurt us the most. That pain runs deep and leaves scars. But it is always reassuring to know that the battle is the Lord's and He's Got Your Back!

"Lord I thank you for always protecting me and having my back. Knowing that the battle is yours, I leave it all to you Lord to help me through the storm and the rain. I give it all to you. Amen."

Personal Thoughts/Reflections

Day 6
Psalms 60:12, NIV
"With God we will gain the victory and he will trample down our enemies."

This is an affirmation. This is as plain and simple as it gets.

"Lord, I take comfort in knowing that my victory comes through you. I am trusting and believing that you will see me through whatever attacks that might come against me. I rest assured in your love for me and I love you for first loving me. Amen."

Personal Thoughts/Reflections

Day 7
Psalms 146:3, KJV
"Put not your trust in Princes, nor in the son of man in whom there is no help."

The arms of flesh will fail you. People will fail you every time but God keeps his promises.

"Dear Father, I thank you for your promises. I thank you for seeing it fit to give me grace without hesitation. In you Lord do I put all my trust, knowing that no weapon formed against me shall prosper. Allow me to never be misguided by others but to rely on you for my directions. Amen."

Personal Thoughts/Reflections

Day 8
Proverbs 21:31, AMP
"The horse is prepared for the day of the battle, but deliverance and victory are of the Lord."

The battle is not yours. Don't stress or worry about it. Turn it all over to God and he will give you the victory.

"Father God, ruler of all creation, I give my all to you. No matter what the circumstances are, I know you will deliver me from all harm and danger and protect me. For these things I give you thanks. Amen."

Personal Thoughts/Reflections

Day 9
Psalms 118:15, NIV
"Shouts of joy and victory resound in the tents of the righteous: The Lord's right hand has done mighty things!"

Once you believe and have faith in God, then you know without the shadow of a doubt that he will perform miracles in your life. He will make the crooked path straight, and he will make things happen that no man can understand.

"Most Faithful Father, Ruler of all Creation, I give you thanks for the mighty works you are performing in my life. I give you thanks for the things that I sometimes take for granted, knowing that I am not worthy, yet you see it fit to bless me. I praise your name above all else. Thank you for giving me the victory. Amen"

Personal Thoughts/Reflections

Day 10
Exodus 15:1, NIV
"Then Moses and the Israelites sang this song to the Lord:
I will sing to the Lord for he is highly exalted. Both horse and driver he has hurled in to the sea."

No matter the odds against you, you have a Savior that will deliver you. Even when things seem impossible to resolve and you are knee deep in some mess, just call on him and he will be there. It may not be on your time but it will be at the right time.

"Heavenly Father, I give you praise for delivering me from dangers seen and unseen. Thank you for showing up when I need you most. Continue to place your shield of protection around me, my family and my loved ones. These mercies I ask in your name. Amen."

Personal Thoughts/Reflections

Day 11
Psalms 21:1, NIV
"The King rejoices in your strength, Lord. How great is his joy in the victories you give!"

Sometimes at your lowest moment is where you find the greatest strength. Strength to get up, pick yourself up, dust yourself off and move because you know that God is in control. Don't give in to defeat, don't give in to failure. They are not of God. Believe in your victory and claim it.

"Dearest God, I trust and believe that you will meet me in this place and give me the victory. I surrender all to you knowing that you rejoice in my victories as well. I praise your name in advance. Amen."

Personal Thoughts/Reflections

Day 12
Revelation 19:1, KJV

"And after these things I heard a great voice of much people in heaven, saying, Alleluia; Salvation, and glory, and honor, and power, unto the Lord our God:"

Nothing lasts forever and there is a time and place for everything. Believing in the power of the Holy Spirit and trusting that God will keep his promises are reassuring.

"Dear God, I thank you for your promises to me, that you will never leave me nor forsake me. I leave all cares at your feet. I glorify and honor your name and worship you in spirit and in truth. Amen."

Personal Thoughts/Reflections

Day 13
1Chronicles 22:13, NIV

"Then you will have success if you are careful to observe the decrees and laws that the Lord gave Moses for Israel. Be strong and courageous. Do not be afraid or discouraged."

As you go through your day, in spite of the what ifs, stay encouraged. God is always close, He never moves. Do not be afraid.

"Dear Lord, I ask that you grant me the strength to endure. Take away the spirit of fear from my heart and replace it with courage. I know that you are always with me. Amen."

Personal Thoughts/Reflections

Day 14
Exodus 23:20, AMP
"Behold, I am going to send an Angel before you to keep and guard you on the way and to bring you to the place I have prepared."

Rest assured knowing that God has a plan for your life and he has a place prepared for you. His Angels are around you standing guard, keeping you, protecting you, until you get to where you are going.

"Lord, today I sing praises to your name and say thank you for sending your Angels to protect me. Guide my feet as I boldly step into the next level of my life, into the place that you have prepared just for me. I am humbled by your Love for me. Amen"

Personal Thoughts/Reflections

Day 15
Psalms 112:8, NIV
"Their hearts are secure; they will have no fear; in the end they will look in triumph on their foes."

Yes, things are not going the way you planned them and you never thought it would be this hard. The enemy is at work in your life, but it is only a matter of time before it is over and you are free.

"Dearest Father, I know the forces are fighting against me, but I have no fear because I know that you are with me and I will defeat the enemy, in Jesus' name, Amen."

Personal Thoughts/Reflections

Day 16
Proverbs 2:7, NJKV

"He stores up sound wisdom for the upright; He is a shield to those who walk uprightly."

Stand firm in your faith, never waiver. Even when you are tempted to fold or give in, stand your ground. God will reward you.

"Father, help me to walk uprightly in spite of my situations. Place your shield around me as a covering. Give me the wisdom to understand and recognize your presence in my life. Thank you for your faithfulness. Amen."

Personal Thoughts/Reflections

Day 17
Genesis 50:20, NLT
"You intended to harm me, but God intended it all for good. He brought me to this position so I could save the lives of many people."

There are times when the very thing someone else meant as harm for you can be turned around for your good. Those unfortunate situations can be a blessing and God has placed you there to bring about a positive change.

"Father God, thank you for the spirit of discernment to understand that this situation that was meant to destroy me, you turned it around for my good. Thank you for the positive change that has resulted in my circumstance and the blessing it has provided for the people around me. Amen."

Personal Thoughts/Reflections

Day 18
Romans 8:28, KJV
"And we know that God causes everything to work together[a] for the good of those who love God and are called according to his purpose for them."

Amen, Amen, Amen. This is a hallelujah scripture and should be an anthem for you.

"Father, I praise your holy name, I magnify you God. I know that you are able to work everything out for my good according to your will. I stand in this promise and in the Love that you have for me. I will continue to walk in my purpose and proclaim my love for you. Amen."

Personal Thoughts/Reflections

Day 19
2 Corinthians 4:7, NIV
"But we have this treasure in jars of clay to show that this all-surpassing power is from God and not from us."

You are powerful beyond measure. God has given you the power to be strong in all things concerning you. Do not give that power away to someone else. It is your birthright from your Father in heaven.

"Father, thank you for equipping me with the Power of the Holy Spirit. When I start letting go or start feeling overwhelmed, may I be reminded that my power comes from you. It is a treasure, it is free and it is all surpassing. Amen."

Personal Thoughts/Reflections

Day 20
2 Corinthians 4:8, NIV

"We are hard pressed on every side, but not crushed; perplexed, but not in despair."

Although the storms may rise, you have an anchor in the Lord. Choose to stay positive, choose to stay prayerful.

"Father God, although my cup is full and running over, although things are coming at me from every angle, I ask that you give me Peace. The Peace that passeth all understanding. Let me stand my ground and not be moved to fear and despair. I count it all as my blessing. Amen."

Personal Thoughts/Reflections

Day 21
2 Corinthians 4:10, NIV
"We always carry around in our body the death of Jesus, so that the life of Jesus may also be revealed in our body."

God sent his Son into this world to die for your sins so that you can have life abundantly. That is the ultimate gift to you.

"Dearest Father, your love for us is so unconditional that you sent your Son to die on Calvary so that we could be saved. I know I don't say it often enough, so right now, in this moment, I just want to say thank you. As a result of that sacrifice Jesus' spirit lives in me. Amen."

Personal Thoughts/Reflections

Day 22
2 Corinthians 4:11, NIV
"For we who are alive are always being given over to death for Jesus' sake, so that his life may also be revealed in our mortal body."

Rest in the fact that God wants us to be Christ like, so that Jesus's life may be revealed in us. What kind of life are you living? Is it pleasing to God? If not, what changes will you make today to receive it?

"Most Holy God, create in me a clean heart. Renew my life from the inside out, so that others can see a Christ like attitude being revealed through me. In Jesus' name, Amen."

Personal Thoughts/Reflections

Day 23
Lamentations 3:24, NIV
"I say to myself, 'The Lord is my portion; therefore, I will wait for him."

Leave it all at the Altar
Leave it all in His hands.
Whatever you desire, whatever you need, let it be known to God and then watch and see the miracle take form.

"Father, you are my portion and I will wait on you. I believe your words for my life and I know you are working on my behalf. In Jesus' name. Amen."

Personal Thoughts/Reflections

Day 24
1 Corinthians 10:13,
"The temptations in your life are no different from what others experience. And God is faithful. He will not allow the temptation to be more than you can stand. When you are tempted, he will show you a way out so that you can endure."

He will not give you more than you can bear. He will provide situations in your life to show you a way out.

"Father, you are a Just and Faithful God. I thank you Lord that you promised a way out of difficult situations. Please take from me any spirit of doubt, anxiety and depression and replace it with belief, peace and hopefulness. Send those people into my life that will feed me with positivity and encouragement in Jesus' name, Amen."

Personal Thoughts/Reflections

Day 25
Romans 8:37, KJV
"Nay, in all these things we are more than conquerors through him that loved us."

You are a child of God and the recipient of his love and grace. As a result of this love and grace you are an overcomer, a winner, a survivor.

"Father God, I thank you for your faithfulness towards me. I praise your name and stand in your grace. I love you Lord and I stand in the knowledge that I am more than a conqueror because of your love for me. Amen."

Personal Thoughts/Reflections

Day 26
Philippians 4:13, KJV

"I can do all things through Christ which strengtheneth me."

This is my favorite scripture and my daily affirmation. You and I are fearfully and wonderfully made. You are self-sufficient in Christ's efficiency and can do any and all things that you put your mind to.

"Father, I am reminded that in you I have all the resources and strength I need to do the things I desire to do, become who I desire to be and achieve the things I hope and pray for. I am sufficient, I am enough, I am an achiever, I am a winner and I can do all things in Jesus' name, Amen."

Personal Thoughts/Reflections

Day 27
Romans 6:14,
"For sin shall no longer be your master, because you are not under the law, but under grace."

If you accept and believe and confess your sins, you are made into a new person. Old things are passed away and you are now covered by the grace of God.

"My Lord and Savior, I thank you for your grace. The grace that restores me daily and washes my sins away. I am constantly reminded of your generosity and your promise, that in spite of my unworthiness you love me enough to bless me with this gift. I am filled with gratitude in Jesus's name, Amen."

Personal Thoughts/Reflections

Day 28
Romans 8:31, KJV
"What shall we then say to these things? If God be for us, who can be against us?"

With God on your side, you are preapproved for his blessings and no man can succeed in destroying you, no matter how they try.

"Father, I believe that things will get better, I believe that you will fix it, I believe that joy will come in the morning. I know you will remove the clouds and make my future brighter and no man can prevent that from happening in Jesus' name. Amen."

Personal Thoughts/Reflections

Day 29
Lamentations 3:22, NLT
"The faithful love of the Lord never ends! His mercies never cease."

Rest assured that the Love of God never ends. He loves you forever.

"Heavenly Father, just as I am, I come to you, grateful for your mercies and unending love. You see it fit to bless me, keep me and love me in spite of my sins. I will forever worship and praise your name, in Jesus' name, Amen."

Personal Thoughts/Reflections

Day 30
Deuteronomy 20:4, NIV

"For the Lord your God is the one who goes with you to fight for you against your enemies to give you victory."

Not everyone will stand up and fight your battles with you. There are times when your family and friends will desert you when things get too hot to handle. But know that your Father in heaven will always be there.

"Father, I thank you for standing by me through this situation. Thank you for showing up and giving me the strength to overcome. The power of your presence has given me the victory in Jesus' name, Amen."

Personal Thoughts/Reflections

Day 31
Romans 8:38-39, KJV

"For I am persuaded, that neither death, nor life, nor angels, nor principalities, nor powers, nor things present, nor things to come,
Nor height, nor depth, nor any other creature, shall be able to separate us from the love of God, which is in Christ Jesus our Lord."

What an amazing confirmation. This verse tells of God's connection to his children through his Love and that nothing can deter that.

"Father, your love and compassion is the anchor in my life. I know that nothing in this lifetime, no matter how bad or good and no matter the circumstances, can ever change the love you have for me. I hold onto this promise, in Jesus' name, Amen."

Personal Thoughts/Reflections

Day 32
Psalms 98:1, NLT
"Sing a new song to the Lord, for he has done wonderful deeds. His right hand has won a mighty victory; his holy arm has shown his saving power!"

I love the Psalms. It is a book of songs from the heart.

"Father, I sing praises to your name. I shout at the top of my lungs in gratitude for all the wonderful things you have done in my life. I am saved by your grace and I have the victory, in Jesus' name, Amen."

Personal Thoughts/Reflections

Day 33
Revelation 15:2, NLT
"I saw before me what seemed to be a glass sea mixed with fire. And on it stood all the people who had been victorious over the beast and his statue and the number representing his name. They were all holding harps that God had given them."

What a day of rejoicing it shall be when God's people stand before him in victory.

"Most Holy Father, I have been through the fire and I have been through the flood but I am grateful that you kept me and through faith I have triumphed, I am victorious and I am still standing in Jesus' name, Amen."

Personal Thoughts/Reflections

Day 34
1 John 5:4, KJV
"For whatsoever is born of God overcometh the world: and this is the victory that overcometh the world, even our faith."

Being born of God, in itself is a victory. Speak this into your life, speak this into your situation, speak this into the atmosphere. You are an overcomer.

"Father God, thank you for the gift of your Son who bought my salvation so that I can be reborn in you and be an overcomer through Faith in Jesus' name, Amen."

Personal Thoughts/Reflections

Day 35
Ephesians 6:10, KJV
"Finally, my brethren, be strong in the Lord, and in the power of his might."

Yes, your days seem dark, your heart hurts, your eyes are swollen from tears, you feel alone and lost. I want to encourage you to be strong, believe and have faith in the power of God.

"Dearest Father, please take this cup of hurt and pain from me and replace it with strength, belief and faith in the power of your might. Surround me with your grace, in Jesus' name. Amen."

Personal Thoughts/Reflections

Day 36
Ephesians 6:11, NLT
"Put on all of God's armor so that you will be able to stand firm against all strategies of the devil."

On the next 6 pages there are 7 verses that speaks specifically to arming yourself against all strategies of the devil.

Now this amour does not mean a metal breast plate and the use of physical weapons. This means that you must have faith in God and study his words for understanding so that you have the knowledge that is necessary to fight against evil.

"Father, I am committed to putting on the whole armor and standing up and fighting against all things that are not of you, in Jesus' name, Amen."

Personal Thoughts/Reflections

Day 37
Ephesians 6:13, NLT

"Therefore, put on every piece of God's armor so you will be able to resist the enemy in the time of evil. Then after the battle you will still be standing firm."

Cont'd
Arm yourself with the shield of Faith, the Helmet of Salvation, and the Sword of the Spirit which is the Word of God. That's how you go into battle to fight against the devil.

"Lord, please prepare me with the wisdom, to do your will. Allow me to use your words to defeat the enemy and any evil that comes against my family and I, in Jesus' name, Amen."

Personal Thoughts/Reflections

Day 38
Ephesians 6:14, NLT
"Stand your ground, putting on the belt of truth and the body armor of God's righteousness."

Cont'd
For every battle, there is a preparation phase. You have to have a plan of action with specific strategies to be successful.

"Lord, I pray for a shield of protection to surround me and my family. Clothe me in your armor so I am adequately equipped to go into battle with you by my side. In Jesus' name I pray, Amen."

Personal Thoughts/Reflections

Day 39
Ephesians 6:15-16, NLT
"For shoes, put on the peace that comes from the Good News so that you will be fully prepared.
In addition to all of these, hold up the shield of faith to stop the fiery arrows of the devil."

Cont'd
You have to be able to stand on those strategies to defeat your foe. You also have to have a plan B. This is your "just in case" plan, so that nothing surprises you. When you are fully prepared nothing comes in the way of your success.

"Father, In the name of Jesus, I speak protection from the forces of the enemy. Prepare my path so that I am equipped to deflect the negative forces in my life and to overcome that which was meant for harm. Grant me your peace. This I pray. Amen"

Personal Thoughts/Reflections

Day 40
Ephesians 6:17, NLT

"Put on salvation as your helmet, and take the sword of the Spirit, which is the word of God."

Cont'd
Studying your Bible, the word of God and praying diligently gives you perseverance for your victory.

"Father God, I ask that you grant me the knowledge and understanding to use your words as my sword and my shield. Plant my feet on higher ground as I walk in your promises. In Jesus' name, Amen."

Personal Thoughts/Reflections

Day 41
Colossians 2:15, NIV

"And having disarmed the powers and authorities, he made a public spectacle of them, triumphing over them by the cross."

Woohoooo, yes, yes, yes. Disarming your enemies based on your victory brings about a sense of triumph. Those people that doubted you, lied on you and deceived you? They will soon look at you in awe of all your blessings.

"Lord, I am thankful for your blessings and for disarming those around me that wishes me ill. I pray your continued guidance over my life, in Jesus' name, Amen."

Personal Thoughts/Reflections

Day 42
Hebrews 13:6, KJV
"So that we may boldly say, The Lord is my helper, and I will not fear what man shall do unto me."

Trusting in the Lord as your source of strength and help. This will allow you to be fearless. No need to fear man when God has got your back.

"Heavenly Father, as I bow before you today, I just want to say thanks. Thanks for being my help, thanks for being there for me through it all. I trust in your love for me and will not fear what any man shall do to me because I know you are with me always, in Jesus' name, Amen."

Personal Thoughts/Reflections

Day 43
1 Peter 5:10, KJV
"But the God of all grace, who hath called us unto his eternal glory by Christ Jesus, after that ye have suffered a while, make you perfect, stablish, strengthen, settle you."

God's grace is sufficient. It gives peace and restores hope and comfort.

"Father, I give you all the glory, the honor and the praise. In you, I've found my courage, my strength, my victory and my peace. Thank you for restoring me, in Jesus' name, Amen."

Personal Thoughts/Reflections

Day 44
Joshua 10:8, NLT
"Do not be afraid of them," the Lord said to Joshua, "for I have given you victory over them. Not a single one of them will be able to stand up to you."

Just like Moses crossing the Red Sea, Daniel in the Lion's Den, David and Goliath. So too, will God give you victory over your life. No man will be able to control your life and defeat you.

"Dearest Lord, I am confident in knowing that the same way you have delivered those before me, that you will also deliver me. I put all my trust in you and know that no man will be able to defeat me, in your Son Jesus' name, Amen."

Personal Thoughts/Reflections

Day 45
John 16:33, KJV
"These things I have spoken unto you, that in me ye might have peace. In the world ye shall have tribulation: but be of good cheer; I have overcome the world."

In order to achieve the ultimate Peace, you must be grounded in God's words and shut out all the noise of the World.

"Father God, you are the reason why I sing. I praise your name Lord, that even in my weakest moments and in my trials and tribulations, I find the courage to sing and be cheerful. I know that I am an overcomer in Jesus' name, Amen."

Personal Thoughts/Reflections

Day 46
James 1:3, KJV
"Knowing this, that the trying of your faith worketh patience."

Stand firm in your Faith and let nothing shake it or take it away. It is easy to let go or lose it when you are being tested but be patient and hold on.

"Dear God, you are my rock and my foundation. I am standing firm in my faith and being patient because I know that as I am being tested, my faith will sustain me. In Jesus' name, Amen."

Personal Thoughts/Reflections

Day 47
James 1:4, KJV
"But let patience have her perfect work, that ye may be perfect and entire, wanting nothing."

Being Patient is to Persevere.

"Father, my life is in your hands. I leave it all to you to keep me patient, so that I may want for nothing. I will wait on your perfect work in my life In Jesus' name, Amen."

Personal Thoughts/Reflections

Day 48
James 1:12, KJV
"Blessed is the man that endureth temptation: for when he is tried, he shall receive the crown of life, which the Lord hath promised to them that love him."

Even when you are in the battle or faced with your toughest challenges, you will be rewarded if you just be still in your mind and spirit and endure.

"Heavenly Father, deliver me from all the temptation that surrounds me. Lay me at the throne so that I may endure these trying times in order to receive the crown of life that you have promised. In Jesus' name, Amen."

Personal Thoughts/Reflections

Day 49
James 1:17, KJV
"Every good gift and every perfect gift is from above, and cometh down from the Father of lights, with whom is no variableness, neither shadow of turning."

You are a gift from God. Walk in your purpose.

"Father, I thank you that every good and perfect gift comes from above. I will let nothing stand in my way of worshipping and praising your name all the days of my life, in Jesus' name, Amen."

Personal Thoughts/Reflections

Day 50
2 Corinthians 2:14, NIV
"But thanks be to God, who always leads us in triumph [as trophies of Christ's victory] and through us spreads and makes evident the fragrance of the knowledge of God everywhere."

God will always lead you into Victory. Be sure to give him the Praise. Share with others the blessings in your life so your testimony can be an inspiration to them.

"Holy and Righteous Father, my God in whom I trust. I will forever thank you and praise your name for giving me the victory. I will spread the goodness of your grace to all who I come in contact with, so that they too may sing your praises and spread the good news of your mercies, in Jesus' name, Amen."

Personal Thoughts/Reflections

Day 51
Ephesians 2:4-5, NLT
"But God is so rich in mercy, and he loved us so much, that even though we were dead because of our sins, he gave us life when he raised Christ from the dead. (It is only by God's grace that you have been saved!)."

How merciful is our God! We are saved by his Grace.

"Father, thank you for your grace and mercy, that while we were sinners you saw it fit to save us through grace. Thank you for the gift of mercy that promises us abundant life, in Jesus' name, Amen."

Personal Thoughts/Reflections

Day 52
Ephesians 2:10, KJV
"For we are his workmanship, created in Christ Jesus unto good works, which God hath before ordained that we should walk in them."

You are a work of Art. You were created, formed and fashioned into His likeness. You are not here by chance you are here for a reason. Embrace the calling for your life and be proud to walk in it.

"Dear Lord, I am your child, created and fashioned into your likeness. I am all that you said that I am and will be all that you intended me to be. Help me to walk confidently in that knowledge and to fulfil the plans for my life. Amen."

Personal Thoughts/Reflections

Day 53
Psalms 146:5, NLT
"But joyful are those who have the God of Israel as their helper, whose hope is in the Lord their God."

The Lord God is your helper. Let this fact fill your life with Joy and Hope for all things good.

"Father, I declare that you are my helper and in you all things are possible. I stand in agreement and count it all joy. I love you forever, in Jesus' name, Amen."

Personal Thoughts/Reflections

Day 54
Isaiah 55:11, KJV

"So shall my word be that goeth forth out of my mouth: it shall not return unto me void, but it shall accomplish that which I please, and it shall prosper in the thing whereto I sent it."

How amazing it is to know that God has plans for you. Everything that is promised will be fulfilled and once it is accomplished, it will be pleasing to him.

"Most Heavenly Father, I am humbled and filled with gratitude to know that all that you promise will come to fruition. Your words will not return unto you void, but it will accomplish the things that pleases you and I will prosper as a result, in Jesus' name, Amen."

Personal Thoughts/Reflections

Day 55
Romans 5:8, KJV
"But God commendeth his love toward us, in that, while we were yet sinners, Christ died for us."

Hallelujah to the heavens. God gave the ultimate sacrifice because of his love for us.

"My God, I cannot make it without you. Without your love, I would be dead in sin without a chance of redemption. But you sent your Son to die for my sins so that I could have eternal life. I open my heart and mind and receive your everlasting Love, in Jesus' name, Amen."

Personal Thoughts/Reflections

Day 56
John 3:16, KJV
"For God so loved the world, that he gave his only begotten Son, that whosoever believeth in him should not perish, but have everlasting life."

Imagine, as a parent, watching your child suffer knowing that he is innocent? Being charged, convicted and killed for a crime you know he did not commit? No sacrifice is as great as the one God endured when he sent his Son to die for our sins.

"Mighty God, Everlasting Father, you have shown us the ultimate love, by sending your Son to die for our sins in order to fulfill your promise of granting us eternal life. Thank you for such a pure gift. Help me to walk uprightly in your Love so that I may receive everlasting life, Amen."

Personal Thoughts/Reflections

Day 57
2 Timothy 1:7, KJV

"For God hath not given us the spirit of fear; but of power, and of love, and of a sound mind."

Fear will cripple you. Fear is not of God. He has equipped you with the spirit of power over your life, to think clearly and make the right decisions. Sometimes you just have to dig deep within yourself to find it.

"Father God, I speak against every attack of the enemy. I speak against the spirit of fear and defeat. Open up my heart and mind that I may receive the power of courage, confidence and love, in Jesus' name, Amen."

Personal Thoughts/Reflections

Day 58
John 8:36, KJV
"If the Son therefore shall make you free, ye shall be free indeed."

This is very straight forward and to the point. Free your mind and your spirit will follow.

"Father, thank you for the spirit of freedom. In your Son's name I am made free. Free from bondage, free from depression, free from illness, free from loneliness, free from anything that prevents me from receiving the Joy of the Lord, in Jesus' name, Amen."

Personal Thoughts/Reflections

Day 59
Hebrews 11:1, KJV
"Now faith is the substance of things hoped for, the evidence of things not seen."

The definition of Faith based on the dictionary is as such, "belief that is not based on proof".
As believers the definition is, "the trust in God and in his promises."
You cannot see it but you know its there because you feel it, you are convicted by it and you have accepted it.

"Lord, I trust in you and believe in your words. I have faith in your Love for me and although I cannot see it, I know in my heart that you are with me and that you hold me in your arms always, in Jesus' name, Amen."

Personal Thoughts/Reflections

Day 60
Philippians 1:19, NLT
"For I know that as you pray for me and the Spirit of Jesus Christ helps me, this will lead to my deliverance."

Through God's spirit all your needs will be supplied.

"Father, I pray your spirit over my life. I know that a change is going to come. I know that you are able to make a way out of no way. I know that you will supply all my needs and deliver me, in Jesus' name, Amen."

Personal Thoughts/Reflections

Day 61
Ephesians 3:17, NLT
"Then Christ will make his home in your hearts as you trust in him. Your roots will grow down into God's love and keep you strong."

Be strong and believe in your heart that Christ dwells there and that God loves you tenderly.

"Father, take me in your arms and hold me close, fill me with the Holy Ghost. I open my heart for Jesus Christ to make his home there, so I can be rooted in strength and love. These mercies I ask, in Jesus' name, Amen."

Personal Thoughts/Reflections

Day 62
Ephesians 3:19, NLT
"May you experience the love of Christ, though it is too great to understand fully. Then you will be made complete with all the fullness of life and power that comes from God."

The nature of God's love gives you knowledge. It completes you and it is enough.

"Holy Father, allow me to experience the Love of Christ, although it may be too great to fully understand. Bless me that I may be made complete with the fullness of life and power that can only come from you. Allow that love to shine through me for others to see the reflection of you. I pray in earnest. Amen."

Personal Thoughts/Reflections

Day 63
Ephesians 3:20, KJV
"Now unto him that is able to do exceeding abundantly above all that we ask or think, according to the power that worketh in us."

You are more powerful than you know. Whatever you ask for you, whatever you desire, whatever you seek in God's name, you will receive through His power working in you.

"Father, I thank you for Peace, Grace, Favor and Love in abundance. I know that all I have to do is ask in your name and you will work in and through me to accomplish that which I ask for, in Jesus' name, Amen."

Personal Thoughts/Reflections

Day 64
2 Corinthians 5:17, KJV

"Therefore if any man be in Christ, he is a new creature: old things are passed away; behold, all things are become new."

Once you are reborn in Christ, you become a new person. There is a shift in your thoughts, actions and deeds. You view your life through different lenses and there is a renewing of your spirit.

"Father, create in me a new spirit. Wash away the sins of the old me, so that my thoughts and actions line up with my new life and new spirit, in Jesus' name, Amen."

Personal Thoughts/Reflections

Day 65
Psalms 31:24, NLT
"So be strong and courageous, all you who put your hope in the Lord!"

Your strength and courage comes from putting your trust and hope in God.

"Heavenly Father, when I think about the goodness of your name I am filled with hope and joy. Thank you for giving me the strength and courage to endure, in Jesus, name. Amen."

Personal Thoughts/Reflections

Day 66
Psalms 18:48, AMP
*"He rescues me from my enemies;
Yes, You lift me up above those who rise up against me; You deliver me from the man of violence."*

God will find you in your mess and rescue you.

"Lord, hear my cry and rescue me from the hands of the enemy. Lift me up Lord above those who are against me. Place a shield of protection around me as I climb my way out of my difficult situation. Deliver me in Jesus' name, Amen."

Personal Thoughts/Reflections

Day 67
Isaiah 55:12, KJV

"For ye shall go out with joy, and be led forth with peace: the mountains and the hills shall break forth before you into singing, and all the trees of the field shall clap their hands."

God promises the fullness of Joy and Peace.

"Lord, I am grateful to you for seeing the best in me. I am encouraged by the peace in my life and that I can rejoice in the joy of your presence, in Jesus' name, Amen."

Personal Thoughts/Reflections

Day 68
2 Timothy 1:4, KJV
"Greatly desiring to see thee, being mindful of thy tears, that I may be filled with joy."

The world is full of chaos and often times we get caught up in it one way or another. Although your circumstance seems like it doesn't stand a chance, God promises you the fullness of Joy and Peace to your life.

"Father, amidst the chaos, the noise and the confusion, I hold firm onto faith, knowing that all my tears will be replaced with joy, as this is your desire for me, in Jesus' name, Amen."

Personal Thoughts/Reflections

Day 69
Psalms 91:2, KJV
"I will say of the Lord, He is my refuge and my fortress: my God; in him will I trust."

I love this Psalm. It is one of my favorite. I remembered being abused by my spouse and needing to find some comfort and hope. I would turn to this scripture every night and read it with my children. It became my prayer for deliverance.

The next 3 pages is a continuation of this Psalm.

"Father, I come before thee, humbly bowed in reverence, asking for you to be my refuge and my strength. I cannot do this without you Lord. In You, I place my trust, my all, in Jesus' name, Amen."

Personal Thoughts/Reflections

Day 70
Psalms 91:5, KJV
"Thou shalt not be afraid for the terror by night; nor for the arrow that flieth by day."

Cont'd
Jehovah-Nissi; The Lord Our Banner. Let the Lord fight your battles.

"Lord, cover me with your banner, so that I will be protected from the wrath of the enemy. Replace my fear with the courage of knowing that you will fight my battles, in Jesus' name, Amen."

Personal Thoughts/Reflections

Day 71
Psalms 91:11-12, KJV
"For he shall give his angels charge over thee, to keep thee in all thy ways.
They shall bear thee up in their hands, lest thou dash thy foot against a stone."

Cont'd
God will send his Angels to keep you and protect regardless of what the enemy tries to do.

"Father, in this space and in this moment I ask that you send your Angels to keep me and my loved ones. Give them charge over my life, so they can hold me up when I am feeling broken. Keep my mind stayed on you Lord, in Jesus' name, Amen."

Personal Thoughts/Reflections

Day 72
Psalms 91:14, KJV
"Because he hath set his love upon me, therefore will I deliver him: I will set him on high, because he hath known my name."

Cont'd
Call on God and he will answer you and deliver you because he loves you.

"Father God, I ask for deliverance. Take this cup away from me and set me free. This is a battle I cannot win without you. Set me on a high place with your Love so that I may be delivered, in Jesus' name, Amen."

Personal Thoughts/Reflections

Day 73
Isaiah 25:8, NLT
"He will swallow up death forever! The Sovereign Lord will wipe away all tears. He will remove forever all insults and mockery against his land and people. The Lord has spoken!"

What a mighty God we serve. One who is always there, who wipes the tears away, no matter how many times we mess up.

"Father God, I thank you that no matter how many times I sin and come short of Your glory, you receive me, forgive me and wipe away my tears. Each time I am renewed and refreshed and all sins are forgiven. Thank you for your mercies and your Sovereignty. I love you Lord, in Jesus' name, Amen."

Personal Thoughts/Reflections

Day 74
Psalms 32:7, NLT
"For you are my hiding place; you protect me from trouble. You surround me with songs of victory."

The Lord God surrounds you with songs of victory. Sing praises to his name.

"Holy Father, in you I am victorious. I am surrounded by your spirit and by your power. You hide me in your Grace and in your Righteousness and fills my heart with songs of salvation. Thank you for your protection in Jesus' name, Amen."

Personal Thoughts/Reflections

Day 75
Joel 2:32, NLT
"But everyone who calls on the name of the Lord will be saved, for some on Mount Zion in Jerusalem will escape, just as the Lord has said. These will be among the survivors whom the Lord has called."

Such a reassurance in knowing that if you call on the name of the Lord you will be saved.

"Father, you are such a forgiving and loving God. For as much time as I call on your name, you have saved me and provided an escape from harm and danger for me. Thank you for leading me to safety and allowing me to survive my fate. Amen."

Personal Thoughts/Reflections

Day 76
Psalms 18:6, NLT
"But in my distress I cried out to the Lord; yes, I prayed to my God for help. He heard me from his sanctuary; my cry to him reached his ears."

He is a patient and just God. He sees the tears and he hears them when they fall.

"Dearest Father, I raise my hands to the heavens and cry out to you to take this wheel. Steer this vessel Lord and pull me from my distress. I stand in Faith that my cries have reached your ears and I am rescued, in Jesus' name, Amen."

Personal Thoughts/Reflections

Day 77
Psalms 18:49, KJV
"Therefore will I give thanks unto thee, O Lord, among the heathen, and sing praises unto thy name."

Give God thanks and praises every day for the things he has done in your life.

"Oh Lord my God, how excellent is your name in all the earth. I give you praise for the things you have done in my life. The things that were meant to keep me down made me stronger. The cross that I once carried, turned out to be a blessing. For this I give you thanks, in Jesus' name, Amen."

Thoughts/Reflections

Day 78
Psalms 69:30,
"I will praise the name of God with a song, and will magnify him with thanksgiving."

Lord, I am filled with Gratitude. Thank you for who you are.

"Lord, I come before you with a heart of thanksgiving. I magnify and glorify your name. I am overwhelmed at your kindness. Fill me with your grace, fill me with your love, my world needs you. Allow me to see you through the wonders of your favor in my life, in Jesus' name. Amen."

Personal Thoughts/Reflections

Day 79
Philippians 4:6, NLT
"Don't worry about anything; instead, pray about everything. Tell God what you need, and thank him for all he has done."

How simple and practical is this verse. Make this your daily conversation with God.

"Father, I need you to supply all my needs according to your riches in Glory. Thank you for what you have done in my life at this point and what you will continue to do. I pray that you will give me the desires on my heart, as you see fit. I pray this prayer in your name, Amen."

Personal Thoughts/Reflections

Day 80
Ephesians 2:8, KJV
"For by grace are ye saved through Faith; and that not of ourselves: it is the gift of God."

It is only through the Grace of God that we are saved. Grace is a gift.

"Loving God, how sweet it is to know that you will never change. Show me your face and fill up this space with your grace, in Jesus' name, Amen."

Thoughts/Reflections

Day 81
Psalms 40:1, KJV
"I waited patiently for the Lord; and he inclined unto me, and heard my cry."

The next 6 pages are specific to Psalms 40, which is known as a devotional Psalm.

Patience is the ability or willingness to suppress restlessness or annoyance when confronted with delay. However, God does things on his time and not on ours. He knows just when to save you.

"Lord, on you, I wait patiently for my help. Hear my voice and help me to be still and know that you are working on my behalf, in Jesus' name, Amen."

Thoughts/Reflections

Day 82
Psalms 40:2, KJV

"He brought me up also out of a horrible pit, out of the miry clay, and set my feet upon a rock, and established my goings."

Cont'd
God is a God of multiple chances. Each time you ask for help, he delivers. Think about a time when you have fallen, who was there to pick you up?

"Father God, you are the Great I am, King of Kings and Lord of Lords. Though the storm may rage and hit against me, you remain the Rock that stands firm by my side to calm those storms. You are my only help out of the darkness and so I put my trust in you, in Jesus' name, Amen."

Personal Thoughts/Reflections

Day 83
Psalms 40:3, KJV
"And he hath put a new song in my mouth, even praise unto our God: many shall see it, and fear, and shall trust in the Lord."

Cont'd
How many times did your friends, family and associates see you down on your luck and walked by? But you kept your faith. You kept praising God even through your brokenness.

"Father, there is a new song in my mouth filled with praises in your name. You kept me and blessed me in spite of my situation. In my brokenness you strengthen me for all to see, in Jesus' name, Amen."

Personal Thoughts/Reflections

Day 84
Psalms 40:11, KJV
"Withhold not thou thy tender mercies from me, O Lord: let thy loving kindness and thy truth continually preserve me."

Cont'd
You remembered God's promises to you. You held on to his truth and you kept praying.

"Lord, I pray that your loving kindness and truth will continue to preserve me. I pray your tender mercies over my life, in Jesus' name. Amen."

Personal Thoughts/Reflections

Day 85
Psalms 40:13, KJV
"Be pleased, O Lord, to deliver me: O Lord, make haste to help me."

Cont'd
Then God, in his infinite Mercy reached down and brought you up out of the pit, out of the den, out of the disaster of your life.

"Father God, I've tried it on my own but I have fallen deeper and deeper into darkness. I need you Lord to pick me up and deliver me as I cannot do it without your arms around me. These mercies I ask in Jesus' name, Amen."

Personal Thoughts/Reflections

Day 86
Psalms 40:16, KJV
"Let all those that seek thee rejoice and be glad in thee: let such as love thy salvation say continually, The Lord be magnified."

Cont'd
Your victory, your deliverance, your favor is a blessing. It proves God's Love. Let others know the goodness of God's grace, so they too shall come to know him.

"Lord God, I thank you for your deliverance. I exalt and magnify your name. Jehovah Jireh, my Provider. How awesome is your love that bought my Salvation. I will continually praise you in Jesus' name, Amen."

Personal Thoughts/Reflections

Day 87
Jeremiah 29:11, NLT
"For I know the plans I have for you," says the Lord. "They are plans for good and not for disaster, to give you a future and a hope."

The Lord has a plan for your life. His plans for you are great. Keep praying for peace and prosperity in your life. He will award that to you.

"Dear God, I am thankful that your plans for me are good. I am excited about a future filled with hope and blessings. I pray for continued peace and prosperity in my life. Thank you for loving me the way you do. I pray in Jesus' name, Amen."

Personal Thoughts/Reflections

Day 88
Romans 12:12, AMP

"Rejoice and exult in hope; be steadfast and patient in suffering and tribulation; be constant in prayer."

Praying is your way of communicating with Him. There is comfort in having a relationship with God through Prayer.

"Father, I come bowed before you in prayer. I am leaving it all on the altar. Today, I ask that you grant me patience and peace through my storms, through my sufferings, through my loneliness, through my hurt, through my pain, through my mess. I believe that it is done and I receive it all in Jesus' name, Amen."

Personal Thoughts/Reflections

Day 89
Luke 11:10, NLT
"For everyone who asks, receives. Everyone who seeks, finds. And to everyone who knocks, the door will be opened."

This is the plain Truth. Just ask, just seek, just knock and you will receive, you will find and doors will be opened to you that no man can close.

"Father, in all things, I give you thanks. You see my wants and my needs. I ask that you grant me the desires of my heart as you see fit. Allow me to find the things in life that you have for me. Guide me to the right door that will open opportunities in your name. Your will be done, in Jesus' name, Amen."

Personal Thoughts/Reflections

Day 90
Romans 5:2, NLT

"Because of our faith, Christ has brought us into this place of undeserved privilege where we now stand, and we confidently and joyfully look forward to sharing God's glory."

Hallelujah, Amen, Amen. What a joy it is to know that your Faith has kept you through it all and that you are now standing in God's promises.

"Father God, with open arms I receive the gift of Victory. No weapon formed against me can prosper. Trials and tribulations will never get the best of me. While the devil is planning his attack you are wiping them out and preparing the way for me to overcome them. The battle is not mine it is always yours. Thank you for granting me Faith that keeps me and sustains me. I stand in your presence filled with Joy in your Grace, praising and thanking you for delivering me. I am Victorious in Jesus' name, Amen."

Personal Thoughts/Reflections

Personal Thoughts/Reflections

Personal Thoughts/Reflections

Personal Thoughts/Reflections

Personal Thoughts/Reflections

Personal Thoughts/Reflections

Personal Thoughts/Reflections

Personal Thoughts/Reflections

Personal Thoughts/Reflections

Personal Thoughts/Reflections

Personal Thoughts/Reflections

Personal Thoughts/Reflections

Personal Thoughts/Reflections

About The Author

JOAN T RANDALL CEO VICTORIOUS YOU

Joan Randall is a Keynote Speaker, Consultant, Life Coach, Thrive Strategist and Best Selling Author. She is Founder and CEO of Victorious You, where they provide resources to Women between the ages of 18-60 that are victims and survivors of Domestic Violence. Through her personal experiences of surviving Domestic Abuse, Joan has developed a 5 step strategy for "Finding a Way Out" and going from Broken to Brave, Victim to Victor and Survivor to Thriver. She provides tips, tools, and strategies through speaking, training, workshops, and seminars that empower Women to become their best self, live their best life and thrive victoriously.

Joan has been featured in several news articles nationally about her Courage in the face of Domestic Abuse. Some of those publications include the South Carolina *Daily News*, *Today's Charlotte Woman*, the *Charlotte Observer* and the New York Magazine, *What's Happening Now*. She has interviewed on several Talk Radio and Internet Radio Shows. She is the Best Selling Author of "90 Days to a Victorious You", a Devotional Journal that inspires readers to write their reflections as they seek a Victorious Life, through the Word of God, Prayer, and Faith. Her book has been featured on Fox News, CNN, NBC, and ABC. She is currently writing her second book "Bags in The Attic, From Broken to Brave". This book tells her personal story of Surviving Domestic Violence and is due in spring of 2016.

Joan has a passion for giving back. She works closely with Safe Alliance, a non-profit organization for Women and Children of Domestic Violence. She volunteers at the Second Harvest Food bank in Charlotte. She supports the Salvation Army, the Susan G Komen Breast Cancer initiatives, the Go Red campaign for Heart Disease and is a Lifetime Sponsor Donor of St Jude's' Children Research Hospital.

She was born in Kingston, Jamaica and migrated to the US in 1989. She is the mother of 3 beautiful daughters and a son. She has three grandchildren. She currently resides in Concord NC with her husband, Bill Randall.